Death

Gail B. Stewart

KidHaven Press, an imprint of Gale Group, Inc.
P.O. Box 289009, San Diego, CA 92198-9009

Library of Congress Cataloging-in-Publication Data

Stewart, Gail B., 1949–
    Death / by Gail B. Stewart.
        p. cm. — (Understanding issues)
    Includes bibliographical references and index.
    Summary: Discusses the subject of death including how to define it,
    how to say good-bye to a loved one, and how people experience
    grief.
    ISBN 0-7377-0949-9
    1. Death—Juvenile literature. 2. Bereavement—Juvenile literature.
    3. Children and death—Juvenile literature. I. Title. II. Series.

HQ1073.3 .S74 2002
306.9—dc21
                                                              2001002308

Contents

A Brother's Death

It happened four years ago, when she was eleven. Even so, Emily remembers every detail. She came home from school and was changing her clothes. She was going to her friend Erin's house to help Erin baby-sit.

But just as she was putting on her shoes, her mother came into her room and sat on the chair by the desk. She looked tired and her eyes were red and puffy.

"My mom said she had something sad to tell me," says Emily. "And I had this awful feeling. It was like everything inside me turned cold. And then she told me that my brother Rick had been killed in a car accident. He was riding his bike along the road, and someone hit him. I remember that my mom looked like she was going to say something else. But she couldn't talk because she started to cry."

That day, says Emily, was the worst of her whole life.

New Questions

That was the first time anyone close to Emily had died. She had thought about death before. A friend from school lost her father to cancer. Other friends had grandparents who had died. But no one she knew had a brother who died.

Her parents were as upset as she was. The pastor from church came and talked a long time. The phone rang almost all night, it seemed. Everyone wanted to know what happened. They wanted to know when the funeral would be. They wanted to know what they could do to help.

The loss of a loved one brings sadness.

Emily remembers lying in bed that night feeling lost. She says her mind was racing; she had so many questions.

"I was thinking about how just one day ago, I had a brother, but now I didn't," she says. "I wondered what would happen to him. I wondered about the person who hit him. I wondered about funerals, and about what happens when you die. Mostly I wondered if I would ever feel happy again."[1]

Chapter One

An Uncomfortable Subject

Death is an uncomfortable subject for most people. No one likes to talk about dying. It makes people uneasy. Even though everyone dies sooner or later, the idea of it makes people feel anxious and afraid.

One of the main reasons is that death is an unknown. No one knows what it feels like to die. No one knows exactly what happens to a person when he or she dies. Doctors may be able to explain why a person dies from a disease or a heart attack, for example. But they cannot explain what goes on when a person is dead. They do not know what people feel when they die. Is it like going to sleep? Do people go to heaven or any sort of afterlife?

People tend to fear things they don't know about. They show their fear in different ways. They might avoid funerals or talking seriously about death and dying. Sometimes they make jokes about dying as a way of easing their fears. For instance, one woman kidded her husband that when she died, she would come back to haunt him. People call this "whistling in the dark." Just as a person might whistle while walking alone at night to make himself feel brave when he isn't, people feel less afraid when they make jokes about death.

Maybe the biggest reason people fear death is because of the sadness that goes with it. When a person dies, it is final. There are no more chances to talk to the person, to laugh, to share memories. The end of a life is sad for the people left behind. Knowing that she would never see her brother again, Emily felt empty and alone.

The idea of death frightens some people.

A Natural Part of Life

There will always be parts of death that are a mystery. However, there are a great many things about dying and death that are *not* mysteries. Learning about these things can make death less frightening. For example, learning about the changes that occur as people get older can help make death seem less mysterious. It also helps to learn about feelings of grief—the sadness when a loved one has died. Funerals honor loved ones who have died, and learning about such ceremonies makes death less strange, too.

The first thing to understand about death is that it is a natural part of life. No living thing will live forever—a person, a spider, a puppy, or a tree. The moment a living thing is born, it begins to age. The final step in that aging process is death.

The length of the aging process varies. For example, an insect called the mayfly lives its whole life in one day. A Labrador retriever lives an average of twelve years. Giant tortoises live the longest of any animal—up to 177 years. Plants, which are also living things, can live far longer than any animal. Scientists say that one tree in California is 4,700 years old!

Aging

But no matter how short or long its life, a living thing ages. Changes happen, making it grow and develop. Puppies become dogs; little saplings grow into trees. Sometimes the changes happen so slowly,

All living things age and eventually die.

it is difficult to notice them. That happened to Ted, who got a puppy last year.

"We got Lucy when she was twelve weeks old—still a puppy," he says. "And to me, she looks the way she always looked. But the other day my mom showed me a picture of Lucy taken the day we got her. I couldn't believe how different she looked!

Probably when you see a dog every day, you don't notice those changes much."[2]

How People Age

The human aging process is a long one, too. A baby born in the United States in 2001 will probably live between seventy and eighty years. A great many changes will happen in that time. Some changes seem very rapid, as during the first year of a baby's life. Others happen very slowly, taking many years to develop.

At the age of twenty, the human body is at its best. The changes that have been happening up till then have made it strong. A person's muscles, bones, and organs work as nature designed them to. In one's thirties, little changes occur. These changes are very gradual, but they are reminders that a person is getting older.

For example, little wrinkles show on a person's face around the eyes and mouth. One's hair might seem a bit thinner. Seeing small print might be more difficult, too. People who never needed glasses before might need them now.

Even more changes show up when people are in their forties, fifties, and sixties. Hair turns gray; skin becomes dry. Brownish spots, sometimes called age spots, appear on the arms and hands of some people. As they age, adults have a tendency to put on extra pounds. Little wrinkles become bigger. Muscles and joints are not as movable as they were at age thirty.

The signs of aging in people show up very gradually.

The Later Stages

As people get older, the changes become more serious. Organs do not work as well and the heart does not pump blood as well as it once did. The digestive system doesn't work as well, either. Over time the body breaks down, until the person finally dies. This breakdown is as natural as any of the other changes along the way.

Even though it is natural, to some people death is an enemy—something to be fought against. Throughout history, people have wondered what it would be like to live forever. They would like a world in which no one ever died. Old age and disease would no longer exist.

At first this may sound like a perfect world. But thinking about it longer, it's clear that it would not work. If living things did not die, there would be no room for future generations. Cities and towns that are busy now would be packed with even more

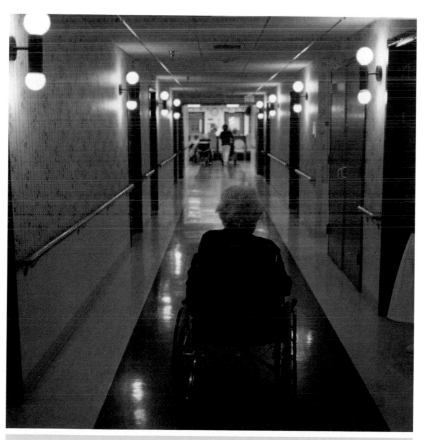

Some wish that old age and death would not exist.

people. Places that are open and wild now would become crowded.

And what would all the new people eat? With no space for farmland, how could enough food be grown to keep people alive? It seems clear that a world like that would never work. Death is nature's way of making room.

Comedian Jerry Seinfeld was on television soon after his daughter was born. He talked about how much he enjoyed being a father. "But let us make no mistake about why these babies are here," he warned, pretending to be serious. "They are here to replace us."[3]

The audience laughed, knowing he was making a joke. However, in a way, he was exactly right.

Young People Die, Too

But there are many people who die for reasons other than old age. Those deaths are harder to understand. People can't say, "She had a nice long life" when a young mother dies in a fire or a young man dies from AIDS. Among adults, heart disease, cancer, and strokes are the leading causes of death.

The deaths of children seem the saddest of all. A six-year-old who is hit by a car has had hardly any life at all. Neither has a twelve-year-old who is shot accidentally. Accidents and cancer are the leading causes of death for children between the ages of five and fourteen.

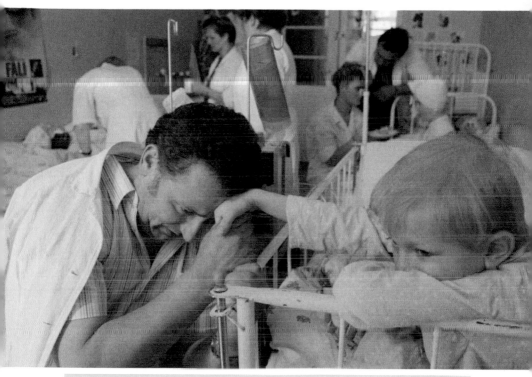

The death of a child seems to be the saddest of all.

Statistics about the causes of death are kept very carefully. Experts want to know how to keep people healthy and safe. People in the United States are lucky; Americans live longer than most of the world's people. But doctors don't have cures for every disease. They cannot repair the injuries of every accident victim. Some people will not get a chance to grow old before they die.

15

Chapter Two

Defining Death

Aaron was six when he found his cat lying at the bottom of the basement stairs. At first he thought she was asleep. He began to pet her but noticed something was very different. The cat's body was stiff. And the cat, who had always purred when he petted her, did not respond.

"I even kept saying her name—Sam—over and over, really loud," he remembers. "But nothing. I went running upstairs to tell my dad. I told him that something was wrong with Sam. He came down and touched Sam, and he knew right away our cat was dead."[4]

The Signs of Death

Years ago, it was just as easy to tell if a person had died. Doctors would listen for a heartbeat or a pulse. They might hold a little mirror or a feather under the person's nostrils. If the feather did not move, or if the mirror did not cloud up, the person was not breathing. With no heartbeat and no evidence of breathing, the person was pronounced dead.

But medicine today is much more complex. Defining death is more complex, too. For example, a heart that has stopped beating can often be restarted. Doctors can use jolts of electricity or strong medicines to start a heart again. And even when a heart is not able to beat on its own, a special machine can do the work.

There are ways of helping a person breathe again, too. Sometimes special machines called **respirators** are used. Other times a lifesaving technique

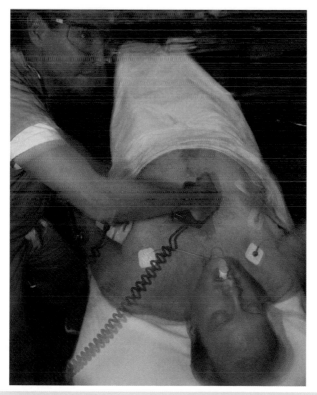

Jolts of electricity can be used to restart a heart that has stopped beating.

CPR can save the life of someone who stops breathing.

called **CPR** (cardiopulmonary resuscitation) can restart breathing. A fireman remembers a little girl who had stopped breathing when she fell into a swimming pool:

> She looked very much like she had died. She had been at the bottom of the pool and no one had noticed for several minutes. She wasn't breathing because she had water in her lungs. Her skin was almost blue, and she was completely still. All firefighters know how to use CPR, and that's what I did. I worked on her for five or

six minutes, I think. All of a sudden, she gagged up some water and started breathing.[5]

Brain Death

Respirators and machines are helpful for an injured or sick person, as long as the brain is alive. But the brain, like the rest of the body, needs oxygen to live. When a person's heartbeat and breathing are stopped for more than several minutes, oxygen cannot get to the brain. Brain cells die, and the brain cannot work. It cannot send out the little electrical charges, called brain waves, that tell the body what to do.

Doctors use a machine to measure how much activity is happening in a person's brain. Every brain wave is recorded on the machine. A healthy brain's graph has many squiggles, showing all of the brain waves. A brain that is not alive results in a straight, flat line. When doctors see a flat line, they know that the person is **brain-dead**.

Brain cells do not repair themselves. Once a brain has died, the person cannot get well. Machines can keep the heartbeat and breathing going, but the person would never really be alive. In these cases, doctors and family members talk about what is best. Usually the machines are turned off and the person is allowed to die a natural death.

Death's Physical Effects

When a living thing dies, it gradually decays, or breaks down into smaller parts. This is easy to see in

A machine can measure how much activity is going on in the brain.

dead plants and grass cuttings. Eventually the little bits of material become part of the soil. This same thing happens to a dead animal or person.

Before it begins to decay, however, obvious changes happen. Just as with Aaron's cat, the body of a dead person is no longer warm to the touch. The skin appears pale and sometimes grayish in color. This is because blood is no longer circulating under the skin.

Dead bodies also seem hard or stiff, too. This results from a reflex that causes the body's muscles to tense. The reflex is called **rigor mortis**—Latin for "stiffness of death." This reflex goes away after twenty four hours or so.

Official Business

Not too many generations ago, when a person died, his family buried him. However, today in the United States, it is required that a doctor examine the body. Afterward, the doctor must fill out an official form called a death certificate. This includes the person's name, the cause of death, and the time and place he or she died. Death certificates are kept by state offices, just as birth and marriage certificates are.

Sometimes there is a question about the death. Perhaps it happened very suddenly, and no one is sure why. Maybe people suspect the person was murdered. Any time there is a question like that, doctors do an **autopsy**. They carefully cut open the body and examine it closely. They look at the various organs. They check blood and tissue under a microscope.

An autopsy can be performed to find out exactly how a person died.

After the autopsy and the cause of death is determined, the organs are put back inside the body. The opening is sewn up, too. The doctor can complete the death certificate. Finally, the body is delivered to a funeral home, where it will be prepared for burial.

"I See My Job as Very Important"

The funeral director has several important jobs. One is working with the family, helping them decide

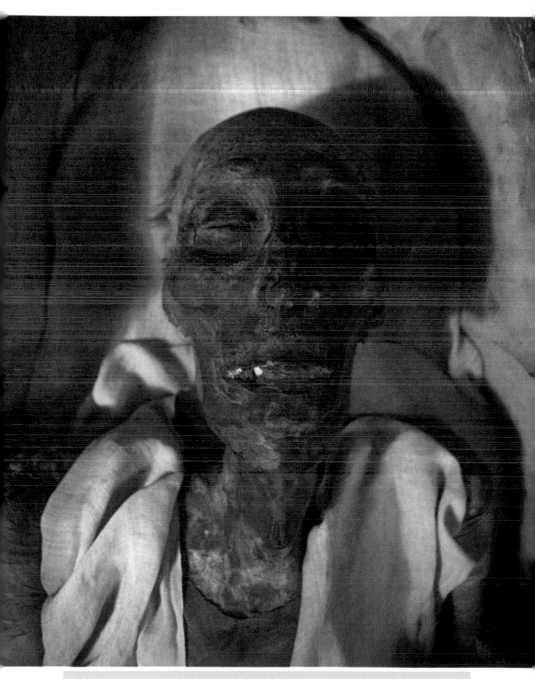

Preparing a body for burial has been practiced for more than eight thousand years.

on plans for a funeral. If the person is to be buried, a long box, or casket, must be chosen. Some are very fancy, made of metal or heavy, polished wood. These may have satin pillows inside and a plush lining. Other caskets are simpler and less expensive. The funeral director also helps the family make a formal announcement, called an obituary. It will appear in the newspaper, telling when and where the funeral will take place.

Another job of the funeral director is preparing the body for burial. Known as **embalming**, this preparation involves removing the blood and replacing it with chemicals. The objective is to slow the decay of the body. This is an old tradition— more than eight thousand years ago, the ancient Egyptians embalmed their dead, too.

People often assume that being a funeral director would be a sad, depressing job. Paul Mallory, a funeral director from Chicago, disagrees. "I always say no," he says. "I see my job as very important. If I've done my job right, if I've paid attention to all the details, I've helped the family in their time of sorrow. . . . My preparing the body for the last time friends and family will see it is a big responsibility."[6]

Chapter Three

Saying Good-bye

The funeral is a very important event. It is the way for family and friends to come together to honor the person who has died. Even though the death of a loved one is sad, a funeral can help people feel better.

When Marlie's grandfather died, she felt very alone. They had been very close—he even taught her how to play the piano. She dreaded going to the funeral. However, she went because her parents wanted her there. To her surprise, it wasn't nearly as sad as she thought it would be. She remembers:

> I saw all Grandpa's friends there. His neighbors and the people from the store where he used to work, too. One of his friends got up and told a funny story about when he and Grandpa went fishing and the motor fell off their boat. It felt funny to laugh but I did. So did everyone else. It was a good way to remember him.[7]

Choices

Funerals often take place in a church or temple. Some are held right in the funeral home, too. The ceremony might include hymns or songs that were favorites of the person who died. There might be prayers or readings. Sometimes the songs and readings are religious, and sometimes not. One teenager says that at his aunt's funeral, a minister read two poems by Robert Frost that the woman had always loved.

I don't think Aunt Rose would have minded something from the Bible, but the poems were the best choice," he says. "She knew them both by heart. I

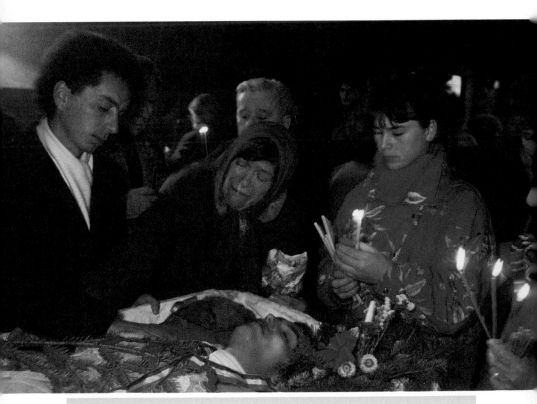

A funeral is one way to say good-bye to a loved one.

know she would have been glad that everyone got to hear them at her funeral.[8]

At the funeral, the casket is in the front of the room. Sometimes it is left open, so people can have a final look at the person who has died. If the person died in a bad accident, he may look much different. For that reason, the family may decide to keep the casket closed. They might put a framed picture of the person on the casket. If the person fought in a war, a flag is often draped on the casket.

At the Cemetery

After the service, the casket is taken to the cemetery. People from the funeral home drive it in a large car, called a **hearse**. The family and friends drive in their own cars, following the hearse. At the cemetery, the casket is carried to the grave, where it will be buried. There might be a prayer or a few words spoken. Often people stand quietly for a few moments, as an act of respect.

The casket is not buried while the people are standing there. That will happen later. However, family and friends may drop a flower or a handful of dirt on the casket. This is a final way of saying good-bye.

Cremation

Many people decide that when they die, they do not wish to be buried in a cemetery. They do not want to be embalmed and placed in a casket. Instead, they prefer that their bodies be cremated.

A casket is carried in a hearse to the cemetery.

Cremation is the disposing of the body by a very hot fire.

This is not a new method. Ancient people in Greece and Rome cremated their dead. So did many people in Africa and India. And long ago, the Vikings set their dead warriors on boats. They would set the boats on fire, before pushing them out to sea.

A body that is to be cremated is placed in a wooden casket. The casket is put into a furnace, which burns at 2,500 degrees Fahrenheit. It usually takes about two hours for cremation. After that, the body has become ashes, with tiny bits of bone. The ashes are put in a special box and are given to the family. The family can decide to bury the ashes in the box. Other times, they keep them in a vase or urn. Sometimes, too, they scatter the ashes in a place that was special to the person.

"We scattered my aunt's ashes in the bird sanctuary near the lake," says Nick. "She was a real bird lover, and that was a good place to see birds all year-round. Whenever I drive by, I think of her."[9]

Why Cremation?

There are several reasons why some people choose to be cremated. Some people believe that the world is getting too crowded for cemeteries. Cities are already short of space. Cremation seems like a good solution to them.

Another reason has to do with cost. Cremations are almost always less expensive than a burial. A body does not get embalmed for cremation. There is no burial plot and no fancy casket to buy. "I know I'll be cremated someday," says one man.

My wife and I have already talked about it. We've got four children. We're not rich. I just can't see spending thousands of dollars on a casket and a burial plot. That adds up. I wouldn't want my wife or kids to have to take that expense on.[10]

Keeping Busy

When Greg's father died last spring, the family worked hard to prepare for the funeral. Relatives from far away had to be called. Greg and his brothers helped their mother with that. They

Although some people wish to be cremated, burial is the choice many prefer.

It is the pallbearers' job to carry the casket from the church to the hearse.

chose music and readings for the service. They chose several of his father's friends to be **pallbearers**, which is considered an honor. Pallbearers are in charge of carrying the casket from the church to the hearse.

Greg says that he was sad about his father's death. However, he did not have time to think about it while he was taking care of the funeral plans. He explains:

31

That was the best thing. We were so busy. The phone was ringing; friends would stop in. There were errands to do. For three or four days, all we did was work! It was so nice having something to do in those first days after Dad died. We couldn't get depressed, because we didn't have time.[11]

Experiencing Grief

The most painful part of a death is the sadness of those left behind. That intense sadness, which is called grief, can make people feel lonely and hopeless. They may wonder how they will ever go on in a normal way.

"I Remember Pretending to Be Sad"

Grief is unpredictable. One person may feel it during the funeral. Another may not feel it for days, weeks, or even months afterward. One girl was twelve when her mother died in an accident. She remembers that she did not feel sad right away:

> That scared me. I thought there was something wrong with me. Instead of feeling sad and crying, I was thinking about who was going to come to the funeral. I was wondering if the other kids in my school would feel sorry for me. I remember pretending to be sad. I didn't really feel grief until a month later, on my thirteenth birthday. That's when all of my sadness came out. I missed her so much,

Grief, or intense sadness, is commonly felt after the death of a loved one.

and I cried a long time. I know now that all of that was normal. I wish I'd known then—I felt so guilty![12]

Feeling Angry Instead

Not everyone cries when they feel grief. Often when a young person loses a family member, he or she might show grief by being angry. This is natural, too. Counselors say anger is a normal emotion to feel.

Andrew's father died in a hunting accident when Andrew was in ninth grade. Soon afterward Andrew began acting different than he normally did. His grades went way down. He skipped classes. He started shoplifting at the mall.

"I see lots of kids like that," says one counselor. "They feel as if they have been abandoned. They're mad at the parent who has died. And those feelings of anger can come out in very strong ways. They may start fights on the playground or stop trying in school. They are miserable for a while, until they can sort out all those feelings."[13]

Honesty Helps

The best thing to do is to talk about the sadness or anger. Talking to a parent or a friend can help. The most important thing is to be honest about those feelings. Trying to act bravely only makes the grief stay longer.

Experts say that honesty helps a lot with very ill people, too. People who know they are dying are often frustrated. They feel that they cannot talk about their death. They might want to talk about funeral arrangements, or about what will become of their things when they die. But death is not a subject their families want to discuss. A counselor explains:

> We don't want to hear about loved ones dying. We want to look on the bright side. We want to hear them say, "I feel better today." But we're cheating them when we don't let them say what they want to say. And we're cheating ourselves, too. We pretend they're going to get well, so we never say good-bye. We never reach for their hands and tell them how much they'll be missed.[14]

Talking about sadness and anger can make people feel better.

"He Wanted to Talk About His Dog"

Sixteen-year-old Michael realized this when his uncle Matt was dying. He had AIDS and was in the last stages of the disease. Matt told Michael that he loved having visitors. But Michael was the only one who did not change the subject when Matt mentioned dying. Michael remembers:

> He told me that everyone else tried to cheer him up. They'd tell him he was looking better, even

though he wasn't. They'd say things like, "Come on, Matt, you'll get through this." My mom even got mad at him once because she said he was getting a negative attitude. But Matt said she didn't mean it. He said she was sad because her brother was dying.

Matt's attitude was fine. He just wanted to talk about real things. I asked him things about his life, about things he wished he'd done. He told me about how he wished he'd learned more about history, and things like that.

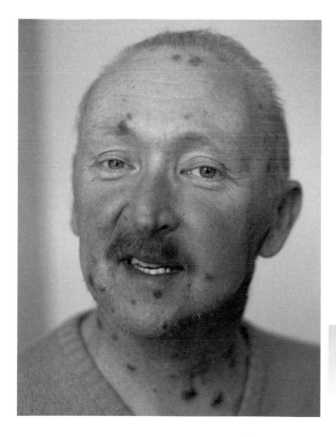

Lesions are a symptom of AIDS.

He always wanted to talk about his dog. He worried that Rip would miss him after he died. Matt worried that Rip would stop eating. He and I talked a lot about Rip, and I promised I'd take good care of him. I know that made him feel better.[15]

A Good Place to Die

Michael was also glad that his uncle did not have to die in a hospital. Matt had told his family he did not want to spend his last days there. It was too noisy, he said. There were too many people coming and going, even at night. Instead, Matt went to a **hospice**.

A hospice is a place for people who are going to die. It is not like a hospital. It is not like a nursing

Many people prefer to die in their own home.

Knowing that death will arrive can make life more meaningful.

home, either. It is more like a real home, with rooms that look cheerful and bright. There are staff workers to help whenever someone needs it. Michael says the hospice was just right for his uncle.

"He didn't have to be in an uncomfortable hospital bed," he says. "Matt had his own sheets and blankets there, and he liked it. We visited, and the staff knew us. They answered questions we had, too. They even let Rip come to visit!"[16]

Things to Think About

As Michael learned, learning about death and dying does not have to be sad. Some schools even offer classes about it. Students learn how different cultures look at death. One boy whose ninth grade

Pallbearers carry a coffin covered with a red tent in a funeral procession in Vietnam.

class was having a unit on death was a little worried. He thought it might be depressing. But it wasn't depressing at all.

"We went to a cemetery and talked to a worker there," he says.

Another time a doctor came in; he told us about working with very sick children. We visited an elder from an Indian reservation, too. He told us how he sings a special song as the dying person gets closer to death. It's supposed to help make their journey to the next world easier. I thought it was the best thing we did in ninth grade.[17]

Learning new things about a subject like death can make it less scary. It is good to know about something everyone will experience someday. And knowing that life *does* have an end makes a person's life that much more valuable.

Notes

Introduction: A Brother's Death
1. Personal interview, Emily, December 3, 1995,
   St. Paul, MN.

Chapter One: An Uncomfortable Subject
2. Personal interview, Ted, April 3, 2001,
   Minneapolis, MN.
3. Quoted in *People Weekly,* April 9, 2001, p. 10.

Chapter Two: Defining Death
4. Telephone interview, Aaron, March 31, 2001.
5. Telephone interview, Gil Watson, March 31, 2001.
6. Telephone interview, Paul Mallory, January 1989.

Chapter Three: Saying Good-bye
7. Personal interview, Marlie, March 23, 2001,
   Minneapolis, MN.
8. Personal interview, Greg, September 16, 1998,
   Bloomington, MN.
9. Telephone interview, Nick, April 2, 2001.
10. Personal interview, Thom, March 30, 2001,
    Minneapolis, MN.
11. Personal interview, Greg, April 15, 1997,
    Richfield, MN.

Chapter Four: Experiencing Grief
12. Telephone interview, Connie, April 1, 2001.
13. Telephone interview, Lynne, March 23, 2001.
14. Lynne, March 23, 2001.
15. Telephone interview, Michael, April 6, 2001.
16. Michael, April 6, 2001.
17. Personal interview, Jerry, February 12, 1999,
    Maple Grove, MN.

Glossary

autopsy: the study of a body to learn about the cause of death

brain-dead: The lack of activity, or brain waves, in a body. Brain death is what tells doctors that a person is truly dead.

CPR: Stands for "cardiopulmonary resuscitation." CPR is a lifesaving technique used on people who have stopped breathing.

cremation: the disposal of a dead body by burning it in a very hot fire

embalming: a way of preserving a dead body by injecting it with chemicals

hearse: A fancy, oversize car used in a funeral to carry the casket.

hospice: a care center for dying people

pallbearers: Friends and family who help carry the casket from the church to the hearse and, later, from the hearse to the grave.

respirator: A machine that can artificially "breathe" for a person whose lungs are not working.

rigor mortis: the stiffening of the muscles after death

For Further Exploration

Audrey Couloumbis, *Getting Near to Baby*. New York: Putnam, 2000. A moving story of two sisters dealing with the death of their baby sister.

Marge Eaton Heegard, *Coping With Death and Grief*. Minneapolis: Lerner, 1990. Readable, with a helpful index and bibliography.

Laurence Pringle, *Death Is Natural*. New York: Morrow, 1991. A good discussion of death in the plant and animal kingdoms.

Elizabeth Richter, *Losing Someone You Love: When a Brother or Sister Dies*. New York: Putnam, 1986. Sixteen young people talk about their experiences and what helped them get through such a difficult time.

Index

Picture Credits

About the Author

Author Gail B. Stewart has written over ninety books for young people, including a series for Lucent Books called The Other America. She has written many books on historical topics such as World War I and the Warsaw ghetto.

Stewart received her undergraduate degree from Gustavus Adolphus College in St. Peter, Minnesota. She did her graduate work in English, linguistics, and curriculum study at the College of St. Thomas and the University of Minnesota. She taught English and reading for more than ten years. Stewart and her husband live in Minneapolis with their three sons.